nature connection

nature connection

a handbook of practices
for therapy and self-exploration

Margaret Kerr & Jana Lemke

Published in this first edition in 2021 by:

Triarchy Press
Axminster, UK
www.triarchypress.net

A catalogue record for this book is available from the British Library.

ISBNs
Print: 978-1-913743-12-3
ePub: 978-1-913743-13-0
PDF: 978-1-913743-14-7

Cover image by Margaret Kerr
Interior illustrations by Margaret Kerr

Acknowledgements

We would like to acknowledge all the teachers who have helped us develop our practice, and in particular Imelda Almqvist, Claudia Goncalves, Mark Halliday, Cris Hofner, Dave Key, Rob Preece, and the School of Lost Borders.

We would also like to express our deep gratitude to the wild lands we have worked in, and the inspiring clients, friends and fellow students we have met through our work. We are forever grateful for the love and support of our closest ones in life, especially Andi and Joe. They have all been our teachers.

Contents

Introduction

As a way of briefly introducing this book we would like to look at an obvious question: why is it beneficial to include nature-connection practices in self-exploration or therapy?

Numerous books have been written about this topic and for those who want to explore the subject more deeply, 'ecotherapy' and 'ecopsychology' may be useful keywords.[1] But we want to keep this handbook an easy read and truly focused on practice.

So here is a short selection of straightforward reasons:

Being outdoors enlivens our sensory perception and helps us to be fully in the present moment – two key elements of mindfulness. Research has shown that cultivating mindfulness has many positive effects on our psychological and physical well-being.

Spending time alone in nature opens up a unique and rare space which often naturally evokes reflections on our personal values and purpose in life. These spiritual aspects of our lives are known to be important factors in human well-being.

But nature does not merely offer a vessel for our reflections, it stimulates and inspires us by being alive, dynamic and interactive. We engage with it and are mirrored by it, but we also get to know a kind of vitality that may not be as present elsewhere in our daily lives. This vitality can inspire future steps in our personal lives.

However, if we look beyond the ideas of 'nature' and 'us', it becomes obvious that we are a part of nature, and that our relationship with the Earth is reciprocal. We cannot exist separately, and what we do as humans has powerful consequences for the ecosystems we are part of.

Experiencing ourselves as part of nature tends to an underlying wound we all carry – a subtle, ever-present feeling of disconnectedness that haunts our current lives and culture.

Recognising ourselves as part of nature opens up a deep sense of belonging to a larger community of life. It can also bring an experience of feeling unconditionally accepted for who we really are.

These changes in our sense of self can then motivate us to start tending the Earth's ecological wounds and rebalancing our part in the web of life.

Who this book is for and how to use it

This is a compact handbook of outdoor practices that can be used by individuals who wish to deepen their own connection with the rest of nature. It is also designed to be used by people who work with others in personal development and healing – for example, coaches, therapists or outdoor educators.

To help ensure that it meets the particular needs of individuals or groups, we have assigned a specific theme, and one or more of five broad categories to each exercise.

The themes suggest which 'life topics' each exercise might help with. However, we believe that each one of us has a unique way of perceiving and responding, and each place that you choose to practise in has its very own story and effect on you and your experience. Therefore, these themes should be understood only as suggestions and not as prescriptive.

The five categories are: Ecological Self, Embodiment, Personal Journey, Mindfulness and Inviting Mystery. These categories suggest which dimension of experience is mainly addressed by each practice. Having said that, they are not mutually exclusive, and most practices can be used to explore several different facets of experience.

Some of the exercises concentrate on empathising with natural elements or a living being and feeling into their innate intrinsic value. We have categorised these as focusing on the **Ecological Self**. The notion of the Ecological Self comes from the writings of the

Norwegian ecophilosopher, Arne Naess.[2] It suggests an experience of deeper interconnectedness and being part of nature, where all parts of the whole have an inalienable right to their own existence.

The category **Embodiment** focuses on bringing awareness to the body and exploring movement in an ecological context and as part of the Ecological Self.

Other exercises invite the practitioner to reflect on their **Personal Journey**. This category together with a particular theme might be useful when looking at personal issues that you want to work on yourself, or in therapeutic or coaching processes with clients.

Exercises in the **Mindfulness** category emphasise exploring the senses, observing the mind and experiencing the present moment.

Finally, **Inviting Mystery** describes exercises that invoke playfulness and creativity, expanding out from the rational everyday world. These experiences may go beyond easy description and invite a taste of mystery into life.

It is always a good idea to draw on your own experience of an exercise before sharing it with others. Alongside this, we hope that the themes and categories will give you extra support in selecting the most relevant exercises for yourself or clients.

This book is a collection of practices that we have found valuable and got to know through our own work, research and spiritual practice. Some have come from the trainings we have undertaken and the teachers we have met. However, we created the majority of the exercises in this book ourselves. We have done our best to reference the original creators of practices and those who shared them with us. But some have been repeatedly passed on and it is sometimes impossible to determine where they originally came from. Where appropriate, to supplement the practices, we have included background notes drawn from our study of other disciplines such as Buddhism, psychology or arts practice.

Being gentle

Going outdoors to practise can be a powerful experience. When we find ourselves alone outside with few distractions, then memories, thoughts, feelings and bodily sensations which have been hidden for a long time can come to the surface. Sometimes, if we have experienced physical or psychological trauma in the past, what surfaces can be distressing. Working outdoors can be a good opportunity to tend to and heal old wounds. However, it is important to be gentle in this process and not to push yourself into painful territory if it does not feel right. It is vital to feel free to be creative and adapt any practice to match your level of physical ability or the locations available to you. Sometimes a lot can be learned from practising in this way.

If anything doesn't feel safe physically or psychologically, there is no shame in pulling back and choosing a gentler path. For example, if you get cold and wet and haven't got enough dry clothing, it's fine to come home early and warm up by the fire. Equally, if you end up feeling lonely and needing someone to talk to, there is no harm in seeking out a friend to share your experience with.

While it is very important to take care of yourself, it can also be helpful to stay compassionately with uncomfortable feelings and watch as they change. For example, often when we have not been in touch with the rest of nature for a while, we can feel alienated as we start spending time alone outdoors. Once we get used to this feeling, we can see it as something temporary that stays until we are able to relax into our surroundings. Just like with an old friend we have not seen for some time, we have to re-approach and reconnect with the wild world inside and outside of us. And then, at some point, timidity or stiffness slowly vanish and something else emerges. In a situation like this, it is worthwhile asking yourself: is this feeling too much for me at the moment, or is it telling me that I am exploring or reclaiming lost terrain? After all, healing means that you have been wounded. So before you know what to heal, you have to be in touch with the wound.

Working with nature is not about conquering what has hurt us or forcing an outcome. Rather, it is about being free to be ourselves, allowing things to emerge when the time is right, and letting nature hold us through this process. Trusting in this will help keep you safe physically and psychologically when working outdoors.

This is very different from the archetypal notion of conquering, or competing with the forces of, nature. The way we tend to our struggles and wounds also applies to our attitude to the rest of nature. We do not go there to test our strength and turn our stay into a survival task. We go respectfully and gently; we listen and respond whenever and however we feel is appropriate.

The power of language

Language affects how we feel and think. Equally, how we feel and think affects the language we use. Terms like 'nature', 'natural world' and 'wilderness' have been the subject of criticism for reinforcing a separation between humans and the rest of the world. Archetypal ideas of 'masculine', 'feminine', 'yin', 'yang' 'animate' and 'inanimate' can be useful in understanding dynamics between elements of the world, but they can also introduce rigid divisions in thinking that are not helpful.

The practices in this book are a chance to go beyond intellectual debates on the use of language, and to rely on personal experience. However, at the same time, they provide a chance to reflect on whether language separates or helps to connect. Your sense of this might change as you keep practising and as cultural understandings and world views shift.

Sometimes it is helpful to use language to draw lines of separation where there are real differences between the elements of the world, and how we interact with them and their needs. But our invitation is to be as conscious as you can of how language is affecting your use of power, and your connection with the world.

Experimenting

Some of the practices in this book involve creative activities that you may feel shy or self-critical about trying, for example singing, movement or drawing. This can be especially true if you have been shamed or criticised for these ways of expression in childhood. If you find yourself feeling shy or critical of yourself in any of these practices, it can help to see them as an experiment, and to remind yourself that nature doesn't judge us for these things.

Some of the practices we have shared are deliberately playful. It is easy to dismiss play as irrelevant to the adult world; however, often the relaxation and fun it brings can be a gateway to a new way of seeing things that has real practical use in our everyday lives.

Our scientific, materialistic culture in the West tends to see the rest of nature as inanimate, or not 'alive' in the same way that we are. Sometimes the practices in this book will work with your surroundings as if they are more conscious or alive than is usually thought. Rather than getting caught up in debates about whether or not this is true, our invitation is to give these practices a go in the spirit of experimentation, and see what happens.

Distractions

There are times when we can distract ourselves unnecessarily due to phantom fears and old habits. For example, sometimes rainy or windy weather can seem like a good excuse not to go out and practice. But it is often in those times when you 'don't feel like it' that the greatest gifts can be found if you do go outdoors.

Another common distraction can come in the form of perfectionism. Diversions like making sure all the chores are done before going out, finding the perfect location to work in, or waiting for the ideal time of day can often sabotage plans, and we can find ourselves not making it out of the door after all!

When you do go out, there are some common distractions that can stop you from fully experiencing the place you are in. Using a phone, reading and making lists can take attention away from awareness of the present moment as it unfolds. Writing, drawing, walking, looking for symbolic meanings in nature and taking photographs can help to deepen an experience, but they can also introduce a subtle distance from what is happening. It can be helpful to develop a sensitivity to when these ways of experiencing are bringing you closer to where you are, and when they are taking you away.

It is often helpful to share experiences of outdoor practice with others when you come home. There are times when it is useful to write down experiences that seem especially significant in a journal, to draw or take photographs: practising outdoors can bring about a different state of mind, a bit like a dream, and subtle experiences can quickly fade with time. However, if you find these methods of recording experience distracting, or if you notice you are mentally 'rehearsing your story', and it is getting in the way of you being present, it is better to let it go, and trust that you will remember what you need to.

Physical safety

Practising outdoors isn't about putting yourself at risk or scaring yourself unnecessarily!

There are some basic things you need to consider to help keep yourself physically safe, and to allow yourself to relax into the practices.

Especially in winter in Northern Europe, the weather can get extremely cold and this is possibly one of the greatest hazards of working outdoors, especially if you are spending long periods of time without moving. Being in the wind, being at high altitude and getting wet will substantially increase your chances of getting cold. Always make sure you take plenty of warm and waterproof clothing, a hat and gloves with you, and wear sturdy waterproof boots. It is better to take more clothing than you think you will need. As you get more experienced at practising outdoors it will get easier to gauge the amount you need to take with you. If you are spending a long day outside, it can be useful to have a sleeping bag and plastic survival bag with you to give an extra layer of warmth. Our bodies can lose a lot of heat through the ground so a polystyrene sit mat or sleeping mat are essential pieces of equipment even for short trips out. If you feel you are getting too cold, it is always better to err on the side of safety. Moving vigorously can help warm you up, but if this is not working, it is better to go home and come back another day.

In other climates, exposure to excessive heat can lead to exhaustion and dehydration. If the weather is likely to be very hot, make sure you've got the right clothing, sunglasses and sunscreen, and take plenty of water to drink. If you are going to be in the same spot for a while, check that you will have access to enough shade as the sun moves round.

If you think there is a chance that you might be out when it gets dark, always take a head torch. Make sure the torch is working before you leave and take some spare batteries. If you have walked a distance to get to where you are practising, time how long it takes you to get there and make sure you leave time to get back before it is dark (unless, of course being out in the dark is part of your plan!). It is helpful to check the time of sunset before you go out.

If you are walking on steep terrain, always make sure that you will be able to get down what you have climbed up. It is a lot easier to climb up than to climb down! If you are in any doubt as to whether you can climb something, don't try it, and choose a gentler route. Equally if you aren't sure that boggy ground will hold you, choose another way to go. Crossing a river on your own, and without training can be dangerous. It's better to make a detour than to find yourself in deep water!

In places that are relatively populated and pastoral, getting lost does not pose too much risk, and can heighten the experience of getting away from our usual routine. But getting lost in mountains or wilderness can tip over into being a stressful or dangerous experience. Always make sure that your ability to navigate matches the terrain you are going into.

If you need the toilet, make sure you go well clear of water sources. Take a small trowel to dig a hole and bury your poo. Moss is a good eco-friendly alternative to toilet paper!

Staying out overnight

Staying out overnight can be a magical and powerful experience. It takes a bit of preparation to make sure you have a comfortable night.

Keeping warm is important as it is easy to cool down while you're asleep. To help with this, always use a foam or blow-up mat to sleep on, as a lot of your body heat will escape through the ground. You will also need a sleeping bag and bivvy bag / tent to help keep you warm and dry. Before you decide where to sleep, have a lie down on the ground and make sure there aren't any tree roots or stones that will poke into you during the night. It is good to choose a spot that is flat, but if you have to sleep on a slight slope, make sure your head is higher than your feet.

If you are using a bivvy bag, put your sleeping mat inside it, otherwise it will drift away under you during the night! Then put your sleeping bag inside the bivvy bag. If you take a small pillowcase, you can stuff your clothes in to make a pillow. If your clothes are wet, take them off and put them in a plastic bag before getting into your sleeping bag. A wet sleeping bag gets cold very quickly.

Sleeping bags are designed to heat up from your body warmth, so it's good not to wear too many clothes so you can start warming yourself up quickly! If you are feeling cold before you get into your sleeping bag, do some star jumps or running on the spot to get warm.

If you're going to spend the night out, take a head torch and spare batteries, and keep it close at hand.

Other people

It isn't unusual to meet others when practising outdoors. Of course, the place you choose will make this more or less likely. If you don't want to be disturbed by getting into conversation, it can be helpful to have a plan for what you will do if you meet someone. Figure out beforehand what will you tell them if they ask what you are doing.

Keep in mind that unexpected encounters with other people are also a matter of perspective. They actually may be an important part of your experience. You can even actively involve people you encounter unexpectedly by asking them a question. Maybe the answer will inform your journey.

Land access laws differ depending on the country in which you are practising. It is worthwhile checking out the access code and permissions for the area you are working in before you go. It is worth remembering that in some areas at some times of the year, people may be hunting or fishing, and access permissions can change.

Wildlife

When we are working outdoors, we are sharing our space with millions of other living organisms. Sometimes we can inadvertently harm them and sometimes they can harm us. It is helpful to educate yourself about local hazards, for example ticks, snakes or poisonous plants, and to observe sensible precautions to protect yourself. However, also be aware that these potential hazards may become an unnecessary focus of anxiety which can divert us from what we went out to explore in the first place!

It is also sensible to become aware of how we can accidentally disturb or harm wildlife in our local area and to be mindful of their habitats. For example, at some times of year it is necessary to avoid areas where there are ground nesting birds or young farm animals. A discussion of this is beyond the scope of this handbook, but there are plenty of online resources which can help you find out what is the best practice in your own area.

Ways of entering a place to practise

Although nature is all around us and we are, ourselves, part of nature, going outdoors to practise is in some ways like entering a different world. Our practice, and the natural world that holds us, can become a sanctuary, and a safe place where transformation can happen.

One thing that we can do in order to strengthen this sense of sanctuary is to cross a physical threshold when we enter the place we have chosen to practise, and to cross back over that threshold when we leave.

A threshold can be anything we choose – an arch made by trees, a gateway, a gap in a wall, a stick broken in two halves and laid on the path before us... When crossing over the threshold at the beginning of the practice, it can be helpful to set an intention. That intention can be as broad or specific as you want. For example, it may be 'To explore my relationship with the rain', 'To get some guidance on my work situation', 'To let go of expectations', 'To remember a friend who has died' or 'To have some time to myself'.

No-one else needs to know your intention. The important thing is that it fits with what you need right now.

Archetypal Journeys and rites of passage

The act of crossing a threshold into the unknown, learning profound lessons, and returning to the mundane world changed, has been identified as a universal pattern of human transformation.

A well-known example is the 'Hero's' or 'Heroine's' journey, but this pattern can be applied to any time in life that involves radical change, like becoming a parent, experiencing a loss or starting a new vocation.[3] It can be helpful to be aware of these transitional phases so we can choose how to enter them consciously.

In some cultures, these journeys are deliberately marked by the community with a ritual called a Rite of Passage.

Ways of processing your experience: alone or with others

Sometimes it is good to go out alone, and to keep your intention and experiences of practice private. At other times, it may be good to go out with friends and practise together. Another way of working together is to ask a friend to 'hold the space' for you while you are out. This might mean sending your friend a message before you go, sharing your intention with them, and telling them of your experiences when you come back. Having your words witnessed non-judgementally can be healing and supportive.

When sharing your experience in a group, it can be useful to hold some kind of object while talking (e.g. a rock, a piece of branch, really anything that you feel is appropriate). This can help focus your attention and ensure that only the person holding it speaks while the others listen. It can also remind listeners to avoid slipping into the habit of commenting, asking questions or sharing their own experiences as a response to what they hear. Once you have finished sharing, you can pass on the object you were holding and the listeners can then reflect back key elements of what they heard.

Hearing a friend's reflections can help you understand what has happened more deeply. Of course, it is important that you choose to share with someone you can trust to respect your experience and perspective. In some traditions, it is usual to 'hold onto' one's experiences for a period of time before sharing them. This acknowledges the principle that things only should be shared when the time is right, so don't feel any pressure to talk about what has happened before you are ready.

Focusing

If you are reflecting a friend's experience back to them, it can be helpful to draw on a technique called 'Focusing'. This is a meditative way of listening and reflecting which was developed by Eugene Gendlin.[4] Learning focusing in depth takes time, patience and practice; there are courses and books which can help if you want to explore this further. But it is relatively straightforward to get started and use some elements of focusing to help a friend process their experience.

For example, if someone says, "I kept walking until I came to the edge of the woods and felt an uneasy feeling", you might reflect back the words 'an uneasy feeling'. This gives your friend a chance to slow down, to think and respond to the deeper content of what they have said. For example, they might agree: "yes, really uneasy!" or refine their understanding: "well, not quite uneasy, more like eerie and uncanny..."

This way of listening relies on reflecting back your friend's exact words, not paraphrasing, interpreting or giving your own impressions. It can help both the speaker and the listener slow down and feel their way towards a deeper understanding.

If you are processing an experience on your own, it can be helpful to 'bring it out into the world' in some way – for example, by drawing, singing, making a clay object, writing or embodying it in movement, making an audio or video recording. It is good to choose the way of expression that you feel most comfortable with. But sometimes, it can also be helpful to record an experience in a way that is unfamiliar. For example, if you usually tend to write things down, you could experiment with drawing or making a video diary instead.

Unusual and mundane experiences

Sometimes when we practise outdoors, we can have extraordinary experiences. Synchronicities may appear that provide answers to long-held questions; we may feel a strong sense of connection with the place we are in, or with the rest of nature. Dream-like states often come and we may have deeply peaceful and healing experiences. Strong feelings come and go – grief, sadness, elation, fear and anger.

At other times, it can feel like nothing has happened. We may go out and feel a bit bored, lacklustre or lonely. Our feet get wet or we get preoccupied with finding a shelter. We can spend ages deciding when to eat the sandwich we have brought with us.

All these things are normal, and there is no one right way for a practice to go. So even if you have a very definite intention when you go out, it's important to hold that lightly and allow whatever happens to take place. Sometimes a relatively mundane event only makes sense when considered afterwards or reflected back by a friend. Sometimes an ordinary experience is just that. The important thing is to be fully present to whatever happens.

Land art[5]

It can be helpful to express what we are experiencing in a place by sculpting with the materials we find around us, for example sticks, stones, sand or natural crevices in rocks. Rather than simply 'using' the materials we find to make a picture, try and enter into a dialogue with them, and be informed by their textures, shapes and properties. In this way, the whole environment becomes a partner in our art practice, and we can open up beyond ourselves to a greater creative force.

Treading lightly

When you find a place you would like to work outdoors, see if you can get a sense of whether this feels right not only for you, but also for the place. The practice you will be doing involves a two-way relationship between you and the plants, animals, birds, rocks and water around you. If you see any evidence that you might be disturbing an animal habitat, or if you get an intuition that you don't feel settled or 'wanted' in a place, it's better to move on and find somewhere else. This isn't to say that you need to find the perfect spot, rather there needs to be enough comfort between yourself and the place to work there. When you have finished working, make sure you haven't left any litter, food or belongings and – like you would if visiting a friend's house – take a moment to thank the place for having you.

If you have made something from natural materials, for example a pile of stones or a circle of sticks, use your own judgement as to whether it feels right to leave it, or to put things back as you found them.

Making a fire without leaving a trace[6]

It is good to make a fire that leaves little trace on the land. To do this, lay a sheet of plastic or cloth where you want to make the fire. Gather some sandy or stony soil (or sand if you're on a beach) and make a mound about 30cm deep on the sheet. Make your fire on top of this mound. Like this, the heat will not penetrate through to the earth beneath and damage tree roots, bulbs, plants or animals living below ground.

Don't burn synthetic materials as they will not burn up completely and could leave a toxic residue. Try and only use as much fuel as you can burn so that everything is reduced to ash when the fire is finished. Ash has a different pH from the rest of the ground, so it is good to dilute it before you put it anywhere. Fortunately this is easily done as you already have a mound of earth to mix it into!

Once the ash is cool, crunch it up among the earth like you were kneading bread. Gather up the ash/earth mixture in the sheet, take it back to the place you got the earth from and pour it back onto the ground.

Giving and taking

Having said that it is good to tread lightly; sometimes you might make or find objects that you want to take home or leave in a place - as an offering, a reminder of your experience or as part of a practice. Perhaps for as long as humans have lived on Earth, we have done this and it seems to be a natural part of how we connect with the world around us. The important thing is that we do this with awareness and respect for where we are.

Dreamtime in wild nature

In many cultures dreaming is used and understood as a way to tap into inner knowledge that is otherwise hard to access. The Okanagan word for 'ourselves' translates as 'the ones who are dream and land together'.[7]

Sometimes, falling asleep when you are alone in nature can be an escape from facing an uncomfortable or scary situation. But done intentionally, it can be a gateway to an inner source of wisdom. Asking for a dream before falling asleep can produce surprisingly accurate guidance on questions we are working with.

However, sleep does not always come to order when you are outdoors! You may plan to sleep in the forest and then suddenly find yourself wide awake and not tired at all. The good news is that you can intentionally enter dreamtime while you are awake. This practice is related to the familiar phenomenon of daydreaming. However, in intentional dreamtime you make a conscious decision to let your mind drift. The outdoor environment can help the psyche tap into a deep evolutionary root. We have a dormant, ancient relationship with the rest of nature, and often the transition to a dream-like state happens quite naturally while we are awake and quiet outdoors. Everything you experience during a waking dream can be as deep and symbolic as in a sleeping dream. The most important thing is the intention that you create around the dreamtime: that you can let go and trust that the right dream will come.

In some indigenous cultures, and in neoshamanism, a regular drumbeat is used to help the mind enter a dream-like state. An audio recording of drumming or playing a drum that you take with you can help to lull your waking mind into a dreaming state. Singing, chanting, moving your body or banging two rocks together rhythmically can have a similar effect, and these methods have the added advantage that they need no equipment!

Practices

The rest of this handbook contains outdoor practices. As described above, we have grouped them into five categories: **Ecological Self**, **Embodiment**, **Personal Journey**, **Mindfulness** and **Inviting Mystery**. The practices in each section are not offered in any specific order, as what will be appropriate at any time will depend on your own situation. However, for guidance, we have included an alphabetical list of themes, alongside the page numbers of relevant practices, at the end of the book. So if you are looking to work with a specific area, say for example, 'transition', 'sense of belonging', or 'relationship with trees', this section will help guide you to what we think are the most relevant practices. We hope this will be useful in finding a practice that fits with what you want to explore.

Ecological Self

F ind a place where you can bury your hands in the earth.

Dig in and feel the texture and temperature of the earth. Smell it, lie on it, roll on it. Let it hold you and press against your body.

Notice how your mind and body responds to this intimate contact with the ground.

Theme: Exploring and cultivating groundedness

Related Categories: Embodiment, Mindfulness

L ie down under a tree.

Turn towards the tree and curl around it with your body.

In time, let a song come from the centre of your body and sing to the tree.

Theme: Exploring interconnectedness

Related Categories: Embodiment, Inviting Mystery

F ind a stone to sit on. Feel the contact of the stone with your body.

Straighten your spine.

Then let the song / sound of the stone gradually rise up through the centre of your body to your throat and sing through you.

Theme: Embodying interconnectedness

Related Categories: Embodiment, Inviting Mystery

Songs from the Land

In many indigenous cultures, singing is integral to being part of nature. In the Highlands of Scotland, before industrialisation, song was a constant accompaniment to working in the fields, fishing, raising children, walking, working with fabrics, relaxing, healing, mourning and spiritual practice.[8] Rhythms and melodies often echoed the elements and the movements and sounds of nature. The land was saturated with song. Even today, on long walks in the Highlands, melodies seem to come into consciousness as if from nowhere, but perhaps they come from the land.

S it facing a tree in the woodland. Spend some time drawing it using black ink and the twigs, grass, leaves, moss, earth and anything else you find round about you on the forest floor.

What are the marks and textures you make like? How does this feel different from drawing with a pencil?

Notice how you feel about the tree before and after drawing. What sensations are you left with when you finish and walk away?[9]

Theme: Slowing down and connecting with a tree

Related Category: Inviting Mystery

Drawing outdoors

It can help to aim to capture the feel or spirit of what you are drawing, rather than trying to make a perfect copy of what you are looking at.

Some practices that can help free us up when drawing are: using the non-dominant hand, drawing with eyes shut, drawing without lifting the pencil from the paper (continuous line drawing), concentrating only on textures, on outlines, on light and shade, or using unfamiliar materials, as in the practice above.

It can also help to draw as if you are playing! Picasso said "It took me four years to paint like Raphael, but a lifetime to paint like a child"

Paint a small stone and leave it as an offering to a place that you love.

Theme: Cultivating gratitude

Offerings

In Tibetan Buddhism, it is common to make offerings to the deities and guardian spirits of a place before a retreat or a meditation practice. These offerings are made in the form of visualised substances in meditation practices: water for washing, water for drinking, lights, incense, candles, perfume, food, music. These are the offerings that would be traditionally given to a traveller when they arrive at somebody's home as a guest. But as well as being visualised in meditation, these gifts are also made in the material world. Bowls of offering substances are laid out on the altar for deities and put outside the meditation hall for local spirits. Offerings can be made while asking a deity for assistance, or in gratitude for the help that a spiritual being has given.

On a windy day, find a spot that calls you. Sit down and close your eyes.

Notice in turn:

- How does the wind feel on your body?

- What instruments is the wind playing: what does it sound like through the trees, the sea, your ears, etc.?

- How does it smell and taste?

Now try to notice all these sensations at once. After a while, open your eyes. Notice where and how you can 'see' the wind, with eyes open and shut. Bring your awareness to the wind's special trait: to be essentially invisible.

Choose one of these questions to reflect on:

- What is the relationship between the intangible wind and tangible, material objects?

- What message did the wind give you?

- Can you think of an example in your own life where something invisible affects your life visibly?

- What invisible and intangible facets of you become visible through relationships with others?

- What is your own relationship with what is invisible?

- How are you expressed through everything else?

- How much do you allow the invisible to be part of your reality?

- How does this relate to your intuition?

You might also like to collect natural objects like shells, rocks, feathers, bark and branches, and with some string create a wind mobile. It can be a reminder of the invisible and intangible facets of life.

Theme: Meeting the visible & invisible aspects of life/self

Related Categories: Personal Journey, Inviting Mystery, Mindfulness

F ind a field of long grass that you can return to over a period of days. Crawl through it on your front.

What do you see when you are moving? When you stop? What associations come up? How does your body feel as it moves across the ground? What stops you in your tracks?

Stand up and look at the trail of your journey.

What is the impression you have left on this place and it on you?

Come back again over the next few days and see whether and how the track that you left has changed.

Theme: Taking the perspective of a small animal and seeing the traces we leave behind

F ind a forest clearing. Sit in the middle of it. Let your eyes meet each bush and tree that borders the clearing and forms the circle around you. What is your first impression of the personality / vibe of each tree? At the centre of the circle, slowly turn around until you have met everyone. How does it feel to be at the centre of attention of this circle of trees? Is there one tree in particular that calls for your attention? What does it have to tell you? Listen deeply.

Sit, stand or lie down. Eyes open or closed. Just be in the present moment with the circle of trees. If you feel safe enough and ready, if you feel you want to give back something special: sing a song to them. Any song that comes to mind. Maybe your song is humming or a melody. Don't be embarrassed or shy. Every sound will be most attentively received without judgement. If you don't want to sing, find another gesture to express your respect and appreciation.

How did you feel throughout this exercise? Was there a development or process you could feel happening? What touched you most?

Theme: Entering into a personal relationship with trees

F ind something outdoors that is dead and alive at the same time. Study it in detail with all your senses and enter into a dialogue with it. How are the live and dead parts useful to it? How does it feel about these parts? See where the conversation leads you. When you are ready, give thanks for the connection you have shared with what you found.

Where in your life is the presence of both what is dead and alive helpful?

What have you learned from what you found, and its way of coping with this duality?

Theme: Investigating relationships between death and life

Related Category: Personal Journey

F ind a spot to start from. Spend some time noticing how this place feels, and your connection to it.

You might want to note what you feel in writing, movement, drawing, sound... Walk 10 paces to the north and pick up an object from here. Return to the centre and place the object at the centre as an offering. Repeat this for each of the eight directions NE, E, SE, S, SW and so on.

When you have visited all the directions, arrange all the objects together into one offering to the place. Spend some time noticing how you are now in this place.

Theme: Connecting with and honouring a place

In an area of woodland, hillside, coast or fields, choose a plant that you can find in different stages of growth e.g. a seed, a shoot, a sapling, a small tree and a mature tree. Study them and get a sense of how this type of plant grows. Once you have a strong impression of this, close your eyes, feel the pattern of growth in your body and express it in movement or in sound.[10]

Theme: Exploring growth and transformation

Goethian science

Goethian science is a method which relies on many hours of close observation of plants and landscapes. Through a process of contemplative watching, drawing and intuition, a picture of organisms and ecosystems, and how they grow and change, is slowly built up. In this way, Goethian scientists aim to understand things 'from the inside', and to experience how the components of an ecosystem interact over time.

U sing your hands, respond to the movements of three or four different branches of a tree. Let it develop into a conversation, or a call and response. As the conversation becomes deeper, allow the movement to spread through your body.

Theme: Exploring interconnectedness

Find a creature outdoors that you usually find unpleasant. This will be different for different people, for example some people are afraid of spiders, others feel repelled by slugs or worms.

Watch what kind of negative thoughts, emotions and bodily reactions come in response to thinking about this creature.

Notice them without judgement. Name them silently.

Now direct your attention towards the beauty and unique life of this animal. Name this silently.

What are your thoughts, emotions and bodily reactions now?

Repeat this exercise with the same or a different creature until you recognise a shift in your perception.

Thank them for helping you with this exercise.[11]

Theme: Exploring the power of judgement

R ub your palms together until they feel warm and alive. Now, reach out your palms until they almost touch another element of nature (a plant, rock, animal, water or earth). Examine the space around them. What does it feel like? What qualities can you make out?

Now turn your attention to thresholds like those between water and land, tree trunk and earth, light and dark. Examine how these areas are related to each other.

Lie down on the ground and try to determine the exact border between yourself and your environment:

Look at a tree. Where does the tree end and where does your vision start?

Listen to a bird. Where is the limit of the bird's song and where does your hearing start?

Breathe. Where does the atmosphere end and where does your breathing start?

Use all your senses.[12]

Theme: Cultivating a sense of connectedness

C hoose a landscape and wander there. Find a threshold and cross it with the intention of connecting with what you feel to be the soul of this place. Listen to the soul of the land — how might it mirror your own soul.

Open yourself to any emotion that arises. These feelings might be difficult or joyful. Whatever feelings come, observe them without controlling, suppressing or judging them.

Now, using the materials you find round about you, make an object or a piece of art which you can give as an offering to the land, to honour the feelings you have experienced.[13]

Theme: Honouring shared feeling

Related Category: Mindfulness

Healing Art

As well as expressing what we feel and notice about the world, making art can help us understand, heal and transform difficult feelings. It can also help acknowledge and celebrate joyful and emotions. Authors such as Imelda Almqvist and Shaun McNiff have written about this process in detail.[14]

G o to a field and find the plant there that gives you the most sense of kindliness and warmth. Observe other species that co-exist with this plant side by side.

What do they and this plant have to say about their co-existence?

How might this be useful for your own life?[15]

Theme: Exploring living in harmony

Related Category: Personal Journey

F ind a present in nature. Examine it closely. Who is this gift intended for?

Remember that the gift might be for yourself, another person, place, animal or plant.

Decide spontaneously what needs to be done with it.[16]

Theme: Practising gratitude

Related Category: Personal Journey

L ook for a wound in nature and create a healing ritual for it.[17]

Theme: Tending wounds in nature

Examples of healing practices or rituals

Healing rituals could involve holding an injured part of a tree, disentangling litter from a plant, making an offering or saying a prayer. Whatever you feel moved to do, it is your wholeheartedness in the action that matters.

In springtime, make or find a threshold and step across it. Look, listen and smell, opening up to all that is around you. Notice how the sun can transform life and help things grow. See if you can let yourself (and any questions you have) open up to this sense of natural transformation. Find a place where you feel safe and at home in the landscape — a 'power spot'. Allow a song, words, a prayer or maybe silence to come from this place.[18]

Theme: Supporting transformation

Related Categories: Personal story, Mindfulness

A power spot

A power spot is a place in the landscape that feels powerful to you, and where you feel safe. It may feel like a sanctuary, energising or peaceful, or just 'right'. It might not be obvious why this place feels that way. Finding this spot is often an intuitive process. In some ways, it may feel as if it 'finds' you, rather than you finding it. The writer Rachael Naomi Remen describes how animals can find this kind of place when under threat: "In bullfighting there is a place in the ring where the bull feels safe. If he can reach this place, he stops running and can gather his full strength. He is no longer afraid... It is the job of the matador to know where this sanctuary lies, to be sure the bull does not have time to occupy his place of wholeness. The safe place for the bull is called the *querencia*... When a person finds their querencia, in full view of the matador, they are calm and peaceful... They have gathered their strength around them." [19]

F ind a beach where you can walk along the junction between the sea and the sand.

Walk back and forward along the line where the two meet, noticing how things change as the tide goes in and out as you walk.

Theme: Exploring time and transition

49 | Embodiment

Embodiment

F ind a tall slender tree that sways in the wind. Lean into it with your back and let it support your weight. Registering its movements with your spine, relax as much as you can. You might want to shift so the tree supports different parts of your spine.

Close your eyes and sense the movements deeper in your body.

How do you feel about this tree? Your connection with it? Does this change with time?

Now experiment with coming slightly away from the tree and standing straight on your own... and then leaning back into the tree again.

Notice what it is like to leave the tree. How does your body respond to parting?

Theme: Finding bodily resonance with a tree

Related Category: Ecological self

G o outdoors on a windy day. Stand facing directly into the wind. Feel the places on your body that the wind touches. Notice any sounds and smells carried towards you by the wind.

Now turn ninety degrees, so the wind comes to the side of your body. Explore how that feels and what sensations it brings.

Now turn so your back is to the wind and explore that.

Finally turn ninety degrees again so your other side faces the wind. What do you notice now?

Turn back again to face into the wind and notice if anything has changed in how you feel.

Theme: Deepening a sensory relationship with the wind

Related Category: Ecological Self

W alk barefoot. Walk through sand, earth, mud, water or on concrete. Walk on whatever crosses your way and you feel drawn to. Let your feet become the headquarters of your body. If you want to be playful draw a face on each of your feet or eyes on each of your toes.

Develop a curiosity for who they are and what they want. Maybe you can even hear them talk to you silently while you are walking. Listen to what they have to say. Feel into each texture you walk across.

Do any memories come when you walk on a certain kind of terrain?

While you walk look at your feet kindly. There is so much to appreciate them for: they have devotedly carried you this far.

Write down or draw any messages or memories from this practice.

You might like to keep your drawing or writing where you can see it (maybe next to your shoe-rack!) as a reminder of gratitude for this often forgotten part of the body.

Theme: Developing a compassionate relationship with the body, and listening to bodily wisdom

Related Categories: Personal Journey, Inviting Mystery, Mindfulness

E xplore a tree with the senses of hearing, touch and smell:

Listen – to the leaves, the branches, put your ear to the trunk and listen in.

Feel – with your hands, your face, your body, your limbs.

Hang from a branch, lean into the trunk. How do your muscles and bones feel?

Smell – the trunk, any moss, leaves, flowers, fruit, the roots.

Theme: Exploring and deepening our relationship with trees

Related Categories: Ecological Self, Mindfulness

F ind a bush that is loose enough to get inside. Make sure you can get right inside so you are completely surrounded by it.

Start swaying gently. Close your eyes. Feel and listen.

See if you can lean into the bush as you sway and feel how it supports and resists your movement.

Theme: Experimenting with support

Related Category: Ecological Self

F ollow the movement of the light on the water.

Let the play of light come into your body and dance with it.

Theme: Embodying light and playfulness
Related Category: Inviting Mystery

Capturing the light

Many painters have tried to capture the qualities of light on water, and many have found this a hard thing to do. The fleeting quality of sparkling light seems to resist being made solid and can highlight our human longing to grasp joyful experiences and make them permanent. The poet William Blake said: "He who binds himself a joy does the winged life destroy. He who kisses the joy as it flies lives in eternity's sunrise."

I n a strong wind, let your body respond to the movements of the wind as it pushes on you, and you on it.

Develop a dialogue, a dance.

Then lie down and let yourself roll in response to the force of the wind, like a leaf being bowled along.

How is it to let yourself be moved like this?

Theme: Entering into a bodily dialogue with the wind
Related Category: Ecological Self

L ie down on your side somewhere earthy, sandy or with loose stones.

Gradually clear away the earth or stones that are uncomfortable or not fitting with your body until you have made a hollow that you fit into comfortably.

Just do it by feel, being guided by your comfort and bodily sensations. How does it feel to lie there in this hollow that is the right shape for you?

Once you have done this, stand up and look at the hollow you have made. What thoughts and feelings come up?

Now fill in the hollow with the stones, sand or earth that you removed in the first place. How does it feel to do that?

Theme: Exploring the feelings of inhabiting and leaving traces

Related Category: Ecological Self

S tand with your feet about shoulder width apart. Close your eyes. Extend your awareness through the soles of your feet, deep into the ground, like roots.

Become aware of the sounds around you. Notice how they come from all directions. Keep the physical awareness flowing through the soles of your feet into the ground – you are rooted.

At the same time let your body start to sway in response to the sounds. Let them pull and push you in different directions like the wind makes a tree sway. Feel the rootedness through your feet as the sounds sway your body.

Theme: Cultivating groundedness

Related Category: Mindfulness

S tand at the edge of a lake and let your awareness spread across the surface of the water.

Once you feel you are there on the surface, let hand movements, body movements and sound come from this place. Allow the sound and movements to settle into the song and movement of the lake as it is at this time.

Come back another time and repeat this practice. See if different songs and movements come.

Theme: Embodying interconnectedness

Related Categories: Ecological Self, Inviting Mystery

Mantra and mudra

In Tibetan Buddhism, mantras (repeated short phrases, that are often sung) are used to connect to the attributes of deities or spiritual beings, for example compassion, discernment, protection or purification. Mudras are hand gestures that are used to express inner states and to embody certain qualities, for example compassion, teaching, or setting boundaries.

B ury your face in the grass. Breathe deeply in and out for a minute or so until your body is flooded with the smell of the grass.

Follow it as it flows through your whole body and its energy starts to move you.

Stay lying on the ground and start to let the movements that come from this experience move your body spontaneously, until it becomes like a dance.

Theme: Embodying interconnectedness

Related Categories: Mindfulness, Ecological Self

F ind a cloud with a definite outline. Imagine that you are climbing around the cloud as if it were a boulder.

Let the movements of climbing come into your body; start to move while you follow the contours around the edges of the cloud with your eyes.

When you have finished, notice if there are any changes in your sense of perspective and the feeling of space around you.

Theme: Embodying a different perspective

Related Categories: Mindfulness, Ecological Self

C lose your eyes. Let your awareness spread down your arms and emerge in the palms of your hands.

Feel / imagine that there are eyes in the palms of your hands.

Open your eyes. Open the eyes in your hands. Start to move and explore – be led by the eyes in your hands. Let the gaze of your usual eyes become soft. Let the eyes in your hands take you to things.

Close your usual eyes. Keep the eyes in your hands open. Move with what you feel / see through them.

Experiment with moving with your usual eyes open or closed whilst always keeping the eyes in your hands open.

Theme: Encouraging embodiment
Related Category: Mindfulness

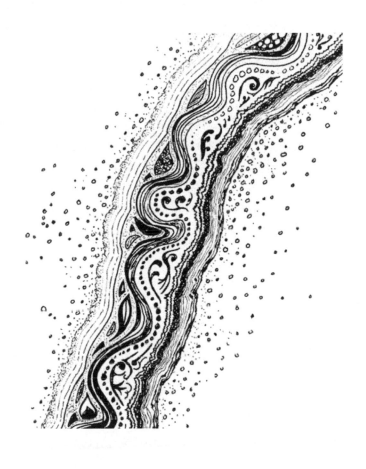

Personal Journey

On the beach near the sea's edge where the tide is coming in, build a circle of sand or seaweed.

Sit with it as the tide comes in and gradually washes it away.

Notice what thoughts and feelings come and go as the tide takes what you have built.

Theme: Being with impermanence

Related Category: Personal Journey, Ecological Self

L ie on the ground on your front. Study the ground in front of you. How does it feel with your hands, how does it look? How does your body feel?

Now roll onto your side and do the same...

Then onto your back and study the sky.

Then onto your other side and do the same...

Then onto your front again. How does your body feel now? Does the ground look the same or different?

Notice each time you change position how you respond to the thought of changing, to the movement of changing and to the new position and view.

Theme: Exploring different points of view

F ind a stone that feels attractive and sit with it in your hand for a while, getting to know its weight, contours, colour and feeling. Let the stone get warm from the heat of your body.

Now throw the stone as far as you can somewhere you can't see it. You might want to close your eyes, throw it behind your back, spin round and let it go, throw it into the undergrowth...

How does it feel to let it go out of your hand?

Now go looking for the stone. What is that like? What thoughts feelings and bodily sensations come up? How do you feel when you find it? Do you want to keep it with you or let it go again?

If you keep the stone, notice when and if you want to let it go and what that process is like.

If you cannot find the stone again, notice how that feels. Stay with those feelings kindly. And find a way to release the stone back to the land compassionately, perhaps with a ritual, a prayer, or a song to say goodbye to it and wish it well.

Theme: Experimenting with holding on and letting go – supporting decision making

Think of something you want to let go of. Find a feather the size of your hand. Stand beside a stream.

Hold the feather cupped in the palm of your hand, thinking of what you want to let go of. Let those thoughts and feelings come into the feather.

When you are ready, let the feather go into the stream.

Watch it as it is carried downstream. If it gets stuck behind a boulder, you might want to free it or leave it be, knowing that time and the flow of the water will eventually carry it away.

Theme: Exploring the process of letting go and surrendering

G o for a walk. Bring to mind someone you want to thank. It may be someone in your life now or from the past, someone well-known to you or not, maybe a person or maybe an animal, or group of people.

As you walk, pick up a stone you feel attracted to – about the size of your palm. As you walk, hold the stone at your heart and bring to mind all you want to thank them for.

Keep carrying the stone, and when more things come, bring the stone to your heart again and visualise the thanks going into the stone. If other thoughts about the person come, let them go for just now. The stone is a carrier of pure thanks.

Keep walking, holding the stone and, when you are ready, place the stone down somewhere you feel drawn to.

Hold the stone with your hand for a few minutes and then continue your walk, leaving the stone in its place.

Theme: Cultivating gratitude

C hoose a spot to start this practice in a
woodland beside an easily identifiable tree.
Now start walking in a straight line (not along a
path). Continue in a straight line for 100-200
metres. Every time a tree, branch, plant or rock
blocks your way, stop. Notice how you feel.

Now look at the 'obstruction' closely for a few
minutes. You might want to explore it by touching
or smelling it. How do you feel about it now?

Now pass the obstruction if you can and continue
walking in a straight line. How do you feel about
passing it and moving on? Do the same each time
something blocks your straight path. Notice how
you feel as the walk progresses.

Sometimes you might need to get down on the
ground to look at something. Also, don't forget
to look up! If something completely blocks your
path, e.g. a stream or large tree, and you have
to turn back 'early', notice how this feels.

Once you have completed 100-200m walking,
turn around and come back the same way,
stopping and noticing, but this time, from a
different angle. How easy is it to recognise and
remember each obstruction? What did you
learn from doing this?

Theme: Dealing with obstacles

Related Category: Mindfulness

F ind a place to sit on the forest floor where there are plenty of twigs and leaves within reach. Set a timer for 10 minutes. Close your eyes and keep them closed. Now, with your hands, start clearing a small circle on the forest floor. When you feel you have cleared a circle, start building twigs and leaves round the outside. Alternate between clearing and building. If you feel like opening your eyes, or start to notice yourself getting bored or rushing, stop, take a few breaths, and slowly start again.

At the end of 10 minutes, open your eyes and look at what you have made. How do you feel about it? Now, with your eyes open, and in your own time, disperse the walls of the circle and cover over the area you have cleared. Notice how you feel doing this.

Theme: Building attachment and letting go

Related Category: Mindfulness

Sand mandalas

In Tibetan Buddhism, mandalas – intricate circular patterns – are made of coloured sand. Monks pour tiny quantities of sand into areas of the circle to gradually build up the image of the mandala. These works take many days to complete, and hours of concentrated work goes into them. Once completed, the mandala is offered up and the sand released into a river. The sand mandala can be seen as a symbol of the intricacy and evanescent beauty of all life.

S pend some time in the woods in amongst the trees. Then go to a clearing or a place just outside of the forest and stay there for some time.

How do you feel inside the forest and outside of it?

Does anything bother or frighten you in each place?

What can you find in each place that is precious to you?

When you've been to both places — which one do you feel drawn to now? How does this connect with your life currently?

Theme: Noticing the resonance between outer and inner spaces

Related Category: Ecological Self

R evisit a natural place that you visited at a memorable time of your life, perhaps a forest, garden, park or cemetery. It may be a few months or years ago or in your childhood. If you can, pick the first place that comes to mind.

On your way, cross a threshold with the intention to let the place bring you back to that time. Let thoughts, images and memories emerge. Maybe allow yourself to get a little lost in your stream of thoughts and images as you walk towards that place. When you arrive, take a moment, pause, and let the echo of your past fade away.

Now come back to the present moment, using your senses. How does this place smell, sound, feel and look now? Alongside this, bring to mind the question: where am I now in my life?

When you feel the time is right, walk back slowly. While you walk, see if you can stay with both the awareness of the place now, and its capacity to hold your memories and life story.

How does this way of remembering change your perception of your past and present life? What does the land mean to you and your life? What has changed, and what has stayed the same?

Theme: Experiencing memory of place and reflecting on change

Related Category: Ecological Self

Think of something you want to let go of. Go for a walk and pick up objects that remind you of this.

Bring the objects back and bind or weave them together.

Then let what you have bound go into one of the elements – earth, water, air or fire.

Do this physically: e.g. make a fire and burn the object, dig a hole and bury it in the earth, let it go into a river, or release it into the wind... [20]

Theme: Letting go

C ross a small stream that you can safely and easily step over in several different ways.

Observe how each way of crossing feels different for you and the stream (and its inhabitants).[21]

Theme: Developing open-mindedness and courage

Related Categories: Mindfulness & Ecological Self

F ind an object or living thing outdoors that catches your attention and repels you. Identify it and become aware of your judgement and what it makes you think. Say it out loud as a criticism. How do you feel now? Look closely and find something that you can potentially love about it. Allow feelings of love to come and stay as long as possible with this loving attention. Express it out loud. How do you feel afterwards?

Notice how it feels to oscillate between aversion and affection. Now turn your attention towards a part of your body that you have a difficult relationship with and repeat this exercise. Make sure that you end the practice with affection.[22]

Theme: Cultivating compassion

Related Category: Ecological Self

Fasting

Fasting contributes to and alters your experience of spending time outdoors in several ways. Research on the effects of fasting during ritualised time alone in the wilderness has shown that it can lead to a variety of physical and psychological changes.

In one study, some participants reported that they felt weaker and slower if they fasted, but some also experienced a boost of energy. Fasting also affected the way they perceived their experiences and surroundings during their solitary time outdoors. A majority started to perceive from a state of calm and switched from a thinking mode to a mode of experiencing and feeling. Interviewees also felt that fasting created a more meaningful space for their time alone as it helped them concentrate on the experience instead of distracting themselves with preparing food and eating.[25]

However, it is important to look after yourself and not to feel that you have to fast. For example, if you have a medical condition, or are on medication, always err on the safe side and check with a doctor first if it is safe to go without food for a day.

This exercise is sometimes called a 'medicine walk' and is based on a practice used by indigenous traditions in North America. It is an intimate time spent alone outdoors from dawn till dusk, in which the practitioner asks for direction to find their inherent gifts: the 'medicine' they bring to the world.

The night before you set off, prepare everything you will need to stay out comfortably and safely for the next day. Decide whether you will take food with you. It sometimes can be helpful to fast while you are out (see below). Let someone know where you are going and when you will be back. It is also good to have a trusted friend welcome you back and to share your experience with them afterwards. Be attentive to the dreams you may have the night before.

Start your walk at dawn by finding a threshold. Remind yourself of the intention you have (to find your 'medicine'), and then step over the threshold. In some native American traditions it is believed that you will attract all the powers of nature which reflect your own medicine. Everything you will encounter is part of a symbolic story which can potentially inform you about your gifts and life path.

Although this practice is often done as a walk,

it is up to you how much you want to move around. You might end up spending a lot of the time you are out sitting or lying down. Most importantly, allow yourself to be led by your intuition. Do not predetermine where you want to go. Just open all your senses like a satellite dish and receive the signals around you. Let the natural world help you to connect with the beauty of life, the reality of death, and everything in-between.

At some point it is likely that you will find something, a symbol of your journey, possibly a symbol of your medicine. Take it home with you.

Arrange to arrive back at your threshold by sunset. Remember that if you have walked a distance, you may need to turn around and start walking back some time before it gets dark. When you reach the threshold, pause a moment, give thanks to the place you have been in, and then step across. Stepping across the threshold marks the moment when you leave one world and come back into another. Whatever you do in this moment, remember to involve your gratitude for the natural world you have been with so intensely during the day. Write down your experiences and share them with a friend.[24]

Theme: Exploring one's life's purpose, self-healing

F ind a natural landscape where you will be
fairly undisturbed. Prepare to go on a walk
back in time towards your birth. It may help to
divide your walk into chunks of 5 or more years, to
remember the sequence of things. It's up to you
how far you want to walk for each chunk.

As you walk back in time pick 3-5 natural objects
(or landmarks) along the way that represent the
most influential moments or periods of your life. If
you can, pick them up and place them prominently
on your path. Don't dwell too much in memories.
You will have time for that on your way back.

Once you reach your birth, sit for a while. Try to
embrace and feel this moment of potential, like a
blank sheet of paper. When you are ready, start
walking towards the present. As you meet the
landmarks/objects you chose. take your time with
each one, pause and feel the importance of these
moments. How did they impact your current
situation, your personality, values and your gifts?

When you reach the present day, see if you can
devise a ritual to make peace with or express
gratitude for your journey and help to affirm your
life in a positive way. Trust that the landscape will
provide the guidance and materials you need to
complete the ritual safely and powerfully.[23]

Theme: Honouring one's life journey, autobiographical work

S tart by finding a threshold. Step across the threshold with the intention to let the playful, creative, inquisitive child that you were, (or could have been) take over.

Make sure you connect with that part of yourself and really let it surface and take over control before you cross the threshold.

Then, take a walk as that child.[26]

To what extent are you still that child? How do you walk, see and understand things differently?

What elements of this are helpful and need more space in your adult life?

Theme: Reconnecting with the inner child

F ind or make a threshold in the landscape and cross it. As you walk, find a wounded part of nature — for example, a plant, tree, animal or piece of land. How does this wound correspond to any elements of your own life? What does it remind you of? Stay with it, spending some time understanding what it has been through. Allow your emotions to come naturally. Now stand alongside the wounded part of nature, and ask yourself, what strength did I gain from this wound?

Give thanks and say good-bye to the injured part of nature. On your way back to the threshold find a symbol that represents the increase in strength you gained from the wound. Take it home with you and cross back over the threshold.[27]

Theme: Reconciling with personal wounds

Make or find a threshold and step across it in the role of a gender that you don't usually identify with.

How do you meet the plants, animals, rocks, water and trees in this role?

What do you want to take with you to your everyday life?[28]

Theme: Exploring gender roles

F ind a natural residential community outdoors. For example, a community of plants, insects, trees or birds.

What are the different roles and relationships you can recognise? Which ones can you most identify with? Which are the ones that you do not identify with?

How can you learn from these roles and relationships, and how might they help you in your everyday life?[29]

Theme: Learning to live in community

L ight a ceremonial fire and become its keeper.

Ask yourself:

Who tended the fire for you?

Who are you tending the fire for?[30]

Theme: Exploring responsibility and care

F ind a wild place that you feel attracted to. Find a threshold and cross it. Connect with this particular landscape. Let your roots run deep.

Now, go back to your line of ancestors. These are not necessarily blood relatives, rather a community of supportive people who went before you, that you feel in some way related to. Who were they? Trust that you are able to connect with more of them than you have actually known or heard of. Let them come. Stay aware of the land while you meet them. You are rooted both in the land and in your line of ancestors.

What do they reveal to you?

Start walking back and collect all the wisdom and gifts you find on your way. Pause before you cross the threshold and feel the abundance of what you gathered.

What do you want to take back home? Find a word or a sentence for your treasure and say it out loud before you cross the threshold.[31]

Theme: Connecting with the ancestors and a sense of belonging

G o for a walk and find objects that can symbolise and express gratitude for four or five things in your life.

Celebrate these parts of your life in a ceremony that you create, perhaps by making something from the objects, holding them in turn, or arranging them in a certain place in the landscape.[32]

Theme: Honouring your life

L ay out a circle of stones or sticks with the points of the compass marked, north, south, east and west.

Step into the circle and face in whatever direction you feel called to. Spend a few minutes bringing to mind a question you would like help with from that direction.

When you're ready, walk out of the circle in that direction to see what you find to help you with your question.

Once you have found what you need, come back into the circle and repeat the practice with each direction in turn.[33]

Theme: Identifying needs and seeking guidance

The Four Directions

In many indigenous and historical traditions, each of the four cardinal directions, North, South, East and West have been associated with different characteristics. These characteristics vary between cultures. To help find your own inner relationship to the four directions, you can go on a journey in your imagination to each direction in turn. Choose one direction, close your eyes and imagine the physical journey to get there. Do you go on foot, in a vehicle, on a bird or animal's back, by sea or by air? When you arrive, what kind of landscape do you find? Notice the colours, textures and sounds, the quality of the air, light and water, and the shapes of the land. What animals, plants and birds have made their home here? What time of day is it, and what season of the year? What age are you while you are here? What is the emotional tone of this place? Is there a call to action or any specific guidance that comes to you? Spend some time looking around and see if there is anything else you notice or feel. When you get a sense that it is time to leave, follow your journey back home, the same way you came. Open your eyes and draw or make a note of what you found. When you are ready you can repeat this process for the next direction, and continue until you have visited all four. It can be useful to find a stone or object that symbolises each direction, and that you can place to mark the cardinal points when you are practising outdoors.

B ring to mind a question or problem that you would like guidance on. Go for a walk, following your intuition about where you go. When you come to a place or an object that catches your attention, stop and look (also listen and touch).

Ask yourself, 'what do I notice?' Once you have run out of things that you notice, then ask the question 'what does this tell me?'

Then when you have completed this enquiry, go back to asking 'what do I notice?' Keep repeating this process until it feels right to stop.

This practice can be very powerful if you do it with a friend. In this case, your friend follows you quietly. When you stop, they stop and ask you the questions 'What do you notice?' and 'What does this tell you?' Your friend just listens while you explore.

Once you have finished the practice, swap over, and do the same for your friend.[34]

Theme: Seeking inner and outer guidance

Related Categories: Mindfulness, Ecological Self

F ind a place in nature where you feel comfortable.

Start collecting natural objects from this place, like sticks, stones or leaves.

Make a piece of land art or a sculpture that reveals your own sense of yourself, as you are right now, in this place. Let the land help you in making this piece of art.

Be guided by the materials you find and the place itself as to how you arrange and connect the pieces together.

Theme: Connecting with your self in nature

Related Category: Ecological Self

Mindfulness

Build a fire and light it. Make sure it is well established, stoked with wood and burning safely.

Now sit by the fire and close your eyes.

What can you sense of the fire without seeing it? Can you sense its smell, its sounds, its warmth? How does that feel in your body and emotionally? Do any memories or associations come? How do these experiences change as you sit? Can you tell without looking if it's time to add wood?

How does it feel to know the fire is there without being able to see it?

Theme: Deepening a sensory relationship with fire, and life energy

Related Categories: Embodiment, Ecological Self, Personal Journey

S tart off walking at your normal pace.

After about 5 minutes halve your pace...
then after another 5 minutes, halve your pace
again.

Each time after you have changed pace for a
while, stop and see how your body, mind and
emotions feel.

Notice what feels good about this practice and
what feels difficult. How does it affect your
relationship with the place you are in?[35]

Theme: Experimenting with personal pace

Related Categories: Embodiment, Personal Journey,
Ecological Self

Walk as quietly as you can for 10 minutes. How do you feel after doing this?

Theme: Becoming aware of our presence

Related Category: Embodiment

Walking quietly

The Vietnamese monk Thich Nhat Hanh has often taught the benefits of walking meditation. He suggests that if we walk quietly and with awareness, we can bring our body and mind into harmony. As our mind slows down and synchronises with our pace, we start to feel our connection with the earth and our surroundings.

F ind an area of forest with no obvious hazards (e.g. ditches, refuse, thorns).

Now get onto your hands and knees and close your eyes. Start crawling and exploring this area only by touch.

You will need to place your hands and knees softly and slowly. Don't be tempted to open your eyes. Rather, feel your way as an insect does, and respond with your body and direction of travel to what meets you.

Theme: Exploring movement and vulnerability

F ind a place where the light falls through the trees, dappling the forest floor.

Sit for half an hour and watch the play of light.

What feelings and reactions come up as the light intensifies, fades and shifts?

Theme: Exploring personal reactions to light

Related Category: Ecological Self

C lose your eyes and become aware of the sounds around you. Notice how they ebb and flow, weave in and out of each other, vary in intensity pitch and tone. Rather than trying to identify them, let them be, and attend to them like you were listening to a piece of music.

Turn your body around to face in different directions. How do they sound now? Lie on the ground and notice how they change.

Walk to a different place and do the same.

Visit different places and experience their soundscapes.

Theme: Exploring the sense of hearing

F ind a place to sit outdoors. Look around and pick up an object with your right hand. Close your eyes and explore it using the sense of touch. How does it feel in your hand? Rub it, hold it, stroke it gently on your hand. Now change it to the other hand and do the same. What do you notice?

Now pick up another object in addition to this – one with a contrasting texture. Hold one object in each hand and explore them alternately and then simultaneously. Bring your hands together and allow any movements to come in the dance between your hands and the objects they are holding. Finally cup your hands and let the objects rest there.

Put the objects down when you are ready. How does it feel to release them? Now open your eyes and look at the objects where they are lying. Notice how this feels and any thoughts that come.

Theme: Exploring the sense of touch

G o for a walk. Preferably on a path or somewhere you can relax. Once you have settled into the rhythm of the walk, turn your attention to the sensations in your body – where your feet touch the ground, the sensations of clothing touching the body, air on the skin, the breath. Keep walking as you do this for 10 minutes.

Now turn your attention to the sounds around you, sounds of clothing, feet, birds, insects, water... for 10 minutes.

Now take your awareness to what you can see – textures, colours, light and shadow – nearby and far away, for 10 minutes.

Now for the last part, spread your awareness to include all that's here – body, breath, sounds and sight for 10 minutes

Theme: Focusing attention

F ind a place to sit outdoors and listen to the sounds around you.

When you are fully immersed in this soundscape, start to draw it. Perhaps draw the soundscape around you for 15 minutes.

 You can compare drawings of soundscapes you make in different places and at the same place at different times of day. What do you notice?

Theme: Deepening sensory experience

Synaesthesia

In synaesthesia, there is a 'crossing over' between different senses. So for example, some people can easily associate colours with certain numbers or letters, while others may 'hear' shapes as well as seeing them. Although not everyone has these kinds of experiences spontaneously, many people find that they can make associations between the senses in practices like drawing the soundscape. Using these kinds of practices can help us to free up connections within our minds and to open up to the world around us in unexpected ways.

F ind a spot to sit outdoors about quarter of an hour before sunset.

Sit in this spot for the next hour or so as the sun sets and the light fades from the sky. Notice the changes in the quality of the light, the air, the temperature, the sky, sounds of birds, animals, trees, traffic.

Do different birds and animals come out as the night falls?

How does it feel to sit still as things change inexorably around you?

Try this practice at different times of year.

Theme: Being with transition from day to night

Related Categories: Ecological Self, Personal journey, Inviting mystery

Mindfulness walk –

Go for a walk and focus on one of these things:
- The sounds round about
- The feeling / sound of your walking
- Your breath
- The air on your skin
- What you can see on the ground
- What you can see at eye level
- The quality of what is underfoot and how the feeling of the ground changes as you walk

Theme: Cultivating awareness

H old your hands out in front of you and look at them.

Gradually spread your arms out to your sides, wiggling your fingers – keep looking straight ahead, while still seeing the movements of your hands. When your hands are only just visible, keep resting your gaze softly like this.

You are now seeing with your peripheral vision.

Stay with this soft peripheral gaze. What do you notice?

Theme: Opening out to a different way of perceiving

S elect seven or eight small stones.

Spend half an hour building them into a pile or other structure.

Notice your challenges and feelings.[36]

Theme: Exploring balance

Related Category: Personal journey

F ind a place to sit. Look around and observe what you can see round about you.

Now build an arch of stones (any size). Spend 10-15 minutes looking through it.

How do you see things differently now? How might this relate to your own life just now?

Theme: Exploring the power of perspective

Related Category: Personal journey

Stone structures

The Inuit people build stone piles called Inukshuks on their land. In Scotland, there is a tradition of building stone piles called cairns. In both cultures, these piles have been used as navigation aids in snowy weather, and as markers of sacred sites. In Inuit culture, it is forbidden to dismantle an Inukshuk.

Without any intention to go anywhere, go for a walk. Keep moving and watch your bodily impulses to change direction as soon as something catches your attention.

Observe any changes in your flow of thoughts when this happens.

Sit on the ground and look ahead. Let your vision become soft, unfocused and blurry.

Observe how changes in what you can see attract your vision and draw the focus of your gaze. Now close your eyes and listen unintentionally. Observe how the sounds around you affect and attract the flow of your awareness.[37]

Theme: Exploring the movements of the mind

G o for a walk.

As you walk, collect objects you find along the way and bring them back.

When you get back, use the objects you have found to make a map of your walk.

Theme: Connecting with a place and starting to feel at home

S it by a stream and close your eyes. Bring your awareness to the ground you are sitting on and feel its solidity. Know that at any time during the practice, if you need to, you can come back to this solidity and feel the ground.

Now let your attention come to what you can hear. Try to hear without naming the sounds, as if you were listening to a piece of music. Let the sounds flow around and through you.

Now open your eyes and watch the movement of the water. Notice the textures, colours and shapes, again without naming if you can. Just enjoy the play of the water and the light. Notice the water's stillness too, and what you can see through it. Then dip your hand in the water. How does it feel on your skin? What happens when you move your hand and play with the surface and the depth.

To finish the practice, bring your awareness to the ground you are sitting on and feel its solidity again.

Theme: Exploring and cultivating fluidity
Related Category: Ecological Self

C lose your eyes and take your awareness to the movements of your breath as it comes in and out of your nose or mouth and fills and empties from your lungs. Spend a few minutes noticing the flow of the breath and the physical sensations it brings in your body. Now open your eyes and open out your awareness to the air immediately around you, from where you draw your breath.

Then let your awareness spread further and further out, noticing the effects of the wind, the clouds in the sky, feeling the air on your skin, and keeping on coming back to your breathing.

Then when you are ready, let go of any specific focus and just be with the breath, the air, the wind and the sky, breathing in and breathing out.

Theme: Exploring and cultivating spaciousness

Related Category: Ecological Self

S it beside a fire outdoors. It can be good to do this at night. First of all have your eyes closed. What can you hear? What can you smell? What can you feel on your skin? Can you feel the heat of the fire? Are some parts of your body warmer than others? What colours and shapes can you see through your eyelids? Now open your eyes and watch the flames and the darkness around. Experiment with moving closer to and further away from the fire, turning sideways on, and turning your back to it, standing up, sitting and lying down next to it. Notice how these changes in your position affect what you take in through your senses.

You can also do this practice in a group in silence. What do you notice as you move closer to and further away from the fire or the rest of the group? It is helpful to come back together as a group and share experiences of this practice around the fire afterwards.

Theme: Exploring the relationship with vital energy
Related Category: Ecological Self

G o out for a walk at night in a landscape where you feel safe. Take a head torch.

At first, walk with your torch on. Notice what you see, hear and how you feel. What thoughts go through your mind?

Now stop and switch your torch off. What do you see and hear now? How do you feel? What goes through your mind? What differences do you notice from when your torch was on?

When you're ready, switch your torch on again, and notice how this is.

Theme: Getting to know the unknown

Related Category: Personal Journey

Inviting Mystery

F ind a blank piece of white card or a blank
sketchbook page (about A4 size) and go
into the woods on a sunny day.

As you walk along under the trees, stop every
few minutes and hold the card out horizontally
in front of you, letting the shadows from the
trees' branches and leaves fall onto the paper.

Notice the movements of the shadows and the
different shapes projected onto the paper –
how do they change with the wind, the time of
day the location and the type of trees around
you?

You might want to take photos of these
'shadow samples'. How does taking photos
change your experience?

Theme: Exploring the ephemeral nature of reality

F ind a place that you feel drawn to –
somewhere you can feel safe and have
privacy to dream. You might want to stay
overnight or to go out during the day with the
intention to sleep. Make a comfortable place to
lie down and surround it with objects that
attract you. You can build a circle or create a
space or shelter with what you find around
you, as the other creatures who live here do.
Spend some time getting to know the plants,
trees and animals around you. Try to meet
them as beings that will help you into sleep
just as a loving parent, grandparent or carer
would with a child. Listen to the lullaby of the
wind and the birds and invite the dream world
your way.

As you wake up, take a pen and paper and
write down or draw what you dreamt or
experienced during this intentional dream
time. If you do not remember any dreams,
write down how you felt when you woke up. If
you were not able to sleep, or were half-asleep,
write down this journey too, and any thoughts
and images that came up.

Take your time to slowly wake up to your
surroundings. Greet them. If you experienced a
very clear image or message during your
dreamtime you might want to say it out loud.
This can help to anchor it in your waking mind.

Thank those around for taking care of you while you were sleeping and take time to put your sleeping area back as you found it.

You might want to tell your experience to a friend when you return and ask for their reflections. Focusing is also a great way to distil the essence of a dream.

Theme: Exploring different states of consciousness

T ake a wind chime and go to the forest. Find a spot to sit or lie down. Create a circle around you and decorate it lovingly. Take your time, this isn't meant to be a simply functional act but part of tuning in with yourself and the world around you. Set up the wind chime in a tree above or beside your circle. Lie down in your circle and ask a question that is close to your heart. Then listen to all the sounds in the forest and the melody of your chime. Don't ruminate or try to form sentences. Just listen and immerse yourself in everything you hear. When you know the time is right, turn your attention towards the question in your heart and see what you can find there. Give yourself time to be grateful for this place with all the living things in it. Carefully disperse the circle you created, returning the pieces to where you found them. What did you feel like after the exercise? What did you find in your heart? How did your perspective or question change?

Theme: Opening up and asking for guidance

Related Category: Personal Journey

S it by a stream.

Put your awareness into the junction between a rock and the water, or the junction between water and air.

Feel the sensation of this junction in your body and move, draw, make something or sing from there.

Theme: Exploring transitional and liminal places

Related Category: Ecological Self

S tand with the sun behind you so you can see your shadow on the ground in front of you. Start moving your hands and put your awareness into the hands of your shadow. Be led by your shadow's hands as they move. Allow your awareness to gradually spread through other parts of your shadow – forearms, elbows, shoulders, neck and so on through to your feet. Be led in your movement by each part of the shadow body as your awareness comes into it.

Theme: Surrendering to a mysterious aspect of self

Related Category: Mindfulness

F ind a feather about 20-30 cm long.

Standing, hold it lightly between your thumb and forefinger, about the height of your solar plexus, pointing ahead of you.

Let it become like the needle of a compass or a dowsing rod. It can pick up subtle currents. Start walking and follow where it takes you.

Theme: Handing over control

I magine that the surface of a lake is the skin of a drum. Play it!

Theme: Encouraging playfulness

G o out at dusk. Let the dusk seep in and sing its song through you.

Theme: Expressing a liminal state
Related Category: Ecological Self

Keywords for themes

Endnotes

1. See for example:

Rust, M.J and Totton, N. (eds) *Vital Signs: Psychological Responses to Ecological Crisis*, Karnac (2012).

and

Roszack, T., Gomes, M.E. and Kanner, A.D. (eds) *Ecopsychology: Restoring the Earth, Healing the Mind*, Sierra Club Books (1995).

2. See for example:

Naess, A., *Ecology, Community and Lifestyle*, Cambridge University Press (1989).

3. Campbell, J., *The Hero With a Thousand Faces*, Pantheon Books (1949); Murdock, M., *The Heroine's Journey*, Shambhala (1990) https://mothernatureproject.org

4. Gendlin, E.T., *Focusing*, Rider (2003).

5. One of the best-known European land artists is Andy Goldsworthy. The film 'Rivers and Tides' shows his way of working.

6. For more information on how to tread lightly outdoors, visit the website https://lnt.org

7. Blackie, S., *If Women Rose Rooted: A Journey to Authenticity and Belonging*, September Publishing (2016) p.354.

8. Newton, M., *Warriors of the Word*, Birlinn (2009).

9. Practice taught by the artist Marged Pendrell.

10. Practice taught by Goethian Science practitioner Roland Playle.

11. This is the first of five exercises taken from the Hawaiian tradition of neoshamanism. They illustrate the 'Huna principles' – principles which are thought to reflect laws of energy that apply to the individual as well as to the Earth.

> The basic intention of these exercises is to help deepen our understanding of life and its all-embracing interconnectedness. The principles are: Ike, Kala, Makia, Aloha and Pono, and refer to thought, energetic connectedness, flow of energy, love and flexibility respectively.

> This exercise works with the Hawaiian Huna principle 'Ike', the power of thought.

12. This exercise works with the Hawaiian Huna principle 'Kala', energetic connectedness.

13. Adapted from Cris Hofner's training materials.

14. Almqvist, I., *Sacred Art: A Hollow Bone for Spirit*, Moon Books (2019); McNiff, S., *Art as Medicine*, Shambhala (1992).

15. Foster, S. & Little, M., *The Four Shields: The Initiatory Seasons of Human Nature*, Lost Borders Press (1999).

16. Adapted from Cris Hofner's training materials.

17. Adapted from Cris Hofner's training materials.

18. Adapted from Cris Hofner's training materials.

19. Kornfield, J., *The Art of Forgiveness, Loving Kindness and Peace*, Bantam (2002) p.184.

20. Adapted from a practice taught by Claudia Goncalves and Mark Halliday of the Edinburgh Shamanic Centre.

21. This exercise works with the Hawaiian Huna principle 'Pono', or flexibility.

22. This exercise works with the Hawaiian Huna principle 'Aloha', the power of love.

23. Modified from an exercise taught by Erika Karman.

24. Foster, S. & Little, M., *The Trail to the Sacred Mountain: A Vision Fast Handbook for Adults*, Lost Borders Press (1984).

25. Lemke, J., *Exploring Human Nature: A Reflexive Mixed Methods Enquiry into Solo Time in the Wilderness*, Sidestone Press (2018).

26. Adapted from Foster, S. & Little, M., *The Four Shields: The Initiatory Seasons of Human Nature*, Lost Borders Press (1999).

27. Adapted from Cris Hofner's training materials.

28. Foster, S. & Little, M., *The Four Shields: The Initiatory Seasons of Human Nature*, Lost Borders Press (1999).

29. Adapted from Cris Hofner's training materials.

30. Adapted from Cris Hofner's training materials.

31. Inspired by Cris Hofner.

32. Adapted from Cris Hofner's training materials.

33. Adapted from a practice taught by Claudia Goncalves and Mark Halliday of the Edinburgh Shamanic Centre.

34. Adapted from practice taught by Mary Jayne Rust and David Key; original practice attributed to Sarah Conn.

35. Adapted from a practice taught by Mary Jayne Rust and David Key.

36. Adapted from a practice taught by Imelda Almqvist.

37. This exercise works with the Hawaian Huna principle 'Makia', the flow of attention.

About the Authors

Dr. Margaret Kerr lives and works in Scotland. She worked as a medical doctor and researcher for 10 years before retraining in psychology, psychotherapy and mindfulness-based approaches to health.

She has practised as a therapist for the past 20 years, and also works as a mountain leader. She runs outdoor mindfulness and nature connection retreats in Scotland.

As well as her therapy work, she is a practising artist and is involved in post graduate study at Duncan of Jordanstone College of Art and Design in Dundee. The focus of all her work is on helping to deepen our connections with the rest of nature.

Dr. Jana Lemke lives and works in Berlin. She trained in psychology and consciousness studies and worked for several years in research, particularly on mindfulness and the human experience of the rest of nature.

She wrote her dissertation on Solo time in nature and trained as an outdoor process-facilitator and systemic therapist. She works as a therapist and co-developed art- and nature-based courses and materials on the significant process of becoming a mother.

Jana's particular passions are working with women and exploring the transformational power of connecting with the more-than-human world.

Margaret and Jana have shared explorations outdoors and worked together on research and writing since 2013.

About the Publisher

Triarchy Press is an independent publisher of books that bring a wider, systemic or contextual approach to many different areas of life, including:

Government, Education, Health and public services

Ecology, Sustainability and Regenerative Cultures

Leading and Managing Organisations

The Money System

Psychotherapy and Arts and other Expressive Therapies

Walking, Psychogeography and Mythogeography

Movement and Somatics

Innovation

The Future and Future Studies

For books by Nora Bateson, Daniel Wahl, Bill Tate, Russ Ackoff, Barry Oshry, John Seddon, Phil Smith, Patricia Lustig, Sandra Reeve, Graham Leicester, Nelisha Wickremasinghe, Bill Sharpe, Alyson Hallett and other remarkable writers, please visit:

www.triarchypress.net